PowerXL Air Fryer Grill Cookbook

Easy, Delicious & Healthy Recipes to Fry, Grill, Bake, and Roast with Your

PowerXL Air Fryer Grill

Branen Classor

Table of Contents

Introduction

Year after year, innovations in technology bring about a new gadget that people go crazy over. And the food industry is no exception.

If you have been spending more time scrolling through your social media feeds or watching television amid the current global pandemic, you have probably caught a buzz on the latest kitchen gadget craze—the air fryer.

This miracle kitchen device can transform almost any food into crispy perfection without the greasiness and mess normally associated with regular frying.

Air fryers are also versatile kitchen appliances, making it an affordable tool for cooking relatively healthier, easier and faster meals. Imagine the space you can save in your kitchen as most air fryers can also grill, bake or roast your favorite meals.

Moreover, air fryers are beginner-friendly and will yield tasty concoctions even with minimal effort. These handy gadgets look after themselves, so to speak. Simply set it up and it will cook your food in at least half the time it normally takes, and then turn off automatically after it's done.

But not all air fryers are created equal. Read on to find out why nothing should stop you from investing in the PowerXL Air Fryer Grill and get experimenting with it at home.

Chapter 1: Overview of PowerXL Air Fryer Grill

What is the PowerXL Air Fryer Grill?

A multifunction air fryer and grill, the PowerXL Air Fryer Grill offers a plethora of menu possibilities with up to 70 percent fewer calories from fat than traditional frying.

It features eight cooking presets that let you air fry and grill at the same time, air fry, grill, bake, toast, broil, rotisserie or reheat food with less cooking oil or none at all. It also does not require thawing and can cook food straight from the freezer.

The PowerXL Air Fryer Grill boasts an up to 450-degree superheated air circulation that ensures the food is cooked evenly on all sides, extra crispy on the outside and tenderly juicy on the inside.

The unit heats almost instantly with a smart preheat feature that starts the timer only when it reaches the desired temperature. It also shuts off automatically.

Equipped with two racks, the PowerXL Air Fryer Grill can cook as much as 4.5 times more food than traditionally smaller air fryers. Ideal for cooking meals for the whole family or when hosting a gathering, the large capacity allows the unit to accommodate up to 10 pounds of chicken, a 12-inch round pizza, six toast slices or bagels, or the equivalent load of a 4.5-quart Dutch oven.

How Does it Work?

In general, air fryers feature a fan that circulates hot air within its chambers in order to cook food. The hot air radiates from the chamber through the heating elements near the food.

To control the temperature, excess hot air is released through an air inlet on the top and an exhaust at the back of the unit.

Instead of being completely submerged in hot oil, food in air fryers are air-heated to induce the Maillard reaction, resulting in browned food with a distinct aroma and taste.

The PowerXL Air Fryer Grill's fan is equipped with turbo blades that are more powerful than its competitors. These blades are angled strategically in order to distribute heat evenly over the surface of the food. Depending on the kind of food, cooking times are reduced by at least 20 percent in comparison with that of traditional ovens.

It also comes with a non-stick grill plate that creates gorgeous grill marks and chargrill flavor without the use of charcoal or propane

Steps to Using the PowerXL Air Fryer Grill

Operating your PowerXL Air Fryer Grill is a breeze with its easy to assemble parts and accessories and simple control panel. After choosing the desired settings, you can just leave it and forget about it until it is time to eat.

Before using the unit for the first time, read all materials, labels and stickers. Remove all packaging, labels and stickers prior to operation. Hand wash all removable parts and accessories with soapy water.

Place the PowerXL Air Fryer Grill on a safe, stable, level, horizontal and heat-resistant surface in an area with good air circulation. Keep the unit away from hot surfaces, other objects or appliances, and combustible materials. It is advisable to plug the unit to a designated outlet.

Carefully assemble the parts and accessories. On the left side of the air fryer's door, you will see guides that indicate the ideal place for the racks and pans. The drip tray should be kept below the heating elements at all times when cooking.

Preheat the unit to allow the manufacturer's protective coating to burn, and then wipe off with a warm moist cloth.

Lightly grease the food before cooking to ensure that it would not stick to the pan or to each other. You may opt to use healthier plant-based oils like avocado and olive. If you are cooking wet food such as marinated meat, pat them dry first to avoid excessive splattering and smoke while cooking.

Avoid overcrowding the food for hot air to circulate effectively and achieve crispy results. Also keep in mind that air fryers cook food faster so follow recommended temperature settings to avoid overcooking or burning.

There are three knobs for: (1) adjusting temperature (up to 450 degrees) and toast darkness options, (2) selecting cooking function (air fry, air fry/grill, grill, broil, pizza/bake, reheat, toast/bagel, rotisserie), and setting the timer (up to 120 minutes).

To make toast, set the toast darkness first and then choose the toast/bagel function. Next, turn the timer knob clockwise past the 20-minute mark, and then rotate counterclockwise to the toast icon.

For the rest of the cooking functions, turn the timer knob past the 20-minute mark before adjusting it to the desired time.

You must select a cooking function for the device to start. When a cooking function and time have been set, the light will turn on. Once the timer expires, the light goes off.

Tips for Care & Maintenance

It is a good practice to visually inspect your PowerXL Air Fryer before each use to make sure that it will function safely and properly. Air fryers may be built to last a long time but just like any other kitchen appliance, you may encounter a few minor and easy-to-fix problems with them from time to time.

Cleaning & Deodorizing

Make sure that the unit is clean before each use. Check the inside for any debris or accumulated dust if you have not been using your unit for some time.

Clean the unit immediately after each use, especially after cooking foods with a pungent smell. Unplug the air fryer and allow it to cool down for at least 30 minutes.

All of the removable parts and accessories are dishwasher safe. If you prefer to handwash, use a mild detergent and soft moist cloth. Do not use abrasive cleaning materials.

Regularly empty the accumulated fat from the bottom of the machine to avoid excessive smoke when cooking.

Storage

After cleaning, make sure that the unit and all its parts and components are dry before storing away. Ensure that the unit will be kept in a stable, level and upright position while in storage. Keep it in a cool, dry place.

Frequently Asked Questions (FAQs)

What is unit size and load capacity of the PowerXL Air Fryer Grill?

The product measures 15.1 x 19.3 x 10.4 inches, with a capacity of 930 cubic inches.

What is the wattage?

1500 watts.

What are the accessories that come with the Air Fryer Grill?

The PowerXL Air Fryer Grill has a grill plate, crisper tray, a rotisserie spit set, a baking pan, a drip tray, and an oven/pizza rack. The deluxe unit also includes a non-stick griddle plate and an egg/muffin tray.

Will the PowerXL Air Fryer Grill help me eat healthier?

The PowerXL Air Fryer Grill uses hot air instead of oil or butter to produce browned and crispy results, creating lower-calorie alternative versions of our favorite deep-fried foods.

What food can I cook in the PowerXL Air Fryer Grill?

You can crisp anything from roasted chicken and steak to potatoes and vegetables. The eight cooking functions can assure you that whether craving classic French fries or corn muffins, your all-in-one air fryer got it all for you.

Chapter 2: Breakfast Recipes

French Toast Strips

Preparation Time: 10 minutes

Cooking Time: 8 minutes

Servings: 6

Ingredients:

- 2 eggs
- ½ cup milk
- ½ cup heavy cream
- ¼ teaspoon ground cinnamon
- ½ teaspoon vanilla extract
- 3 tablespoons sugar
- Pinch salt
- 6 slices loaf bread, sliced into strips

Method:

1. Beat the eggs in a bowl.
2. Stir in the milk, cream, cinnamon, vanilla, sugar and salt.
3. Coat bread strips with the mixture.
4. Place in the air fryer.
5. Set it to air fry/grill.
6. Set it to 375 degrees F.
7. Cook for 4 minutes per side.

Serving Suggestions: Serve with maple syrup.

Preparation & Cooking Tips: Use day-old bread.

Egg Sandwich

Preparation Time: 10 minutes

Cooking Time: 16 minutes

Servings: 4

Ingredients:

- 4 eggs
- 1 cup light mayonnaise
- 1 tablespoon chopped chives
- Pepper to taste
- 8 slices loaf bread

Method:

1. Add the eggs to the air fryer rack.
2. Select air fry function.
3. Set it to 250 degrees F.
4. Cook for 16 minutes.
5. Place the eggs in a bowl with ice water.
6. Peel and transfer to another bowl.
7. Mash the eggs with a fork.
8. Stir in the mayo, chives and pepper.
9. Spread mixture on bread and top with another bread to make a sandwich.

Serving Suggestions: Toast the sandwich before serving.

Preparation & Cooking Tips: Use whole wheat bread slices.

Bagel

Preparation Time: 10 minutes

Cooking Time: 15 minutes

Servings: 4

Ingredients:

- 1 cup all purpose flour
- 2 teaspoons baking powder
- ½ teaspoon salt
- 1 cup nonfat Greek yogurt
- 1 egg, beaten

Method:

1. In a bowl, mix all the ingredients.
2. Knead the mixture.
3. Divide the dough into 4.
4. Roll into a thick rope and then form a bagel.
5. Brush the top with egg.
6. Choose bake setting in the air fryer grill.
7. Set it to 280 degrees F.
8. Cook for 15 minutes.

Serving Suggestions: Brush bagels with egg wash and top with poppy seeds.

Preparation & Cooking Tips: Use whole wheat flour if possible.

Omelette

Preparation Time: 10 minutes

Cooking Time: 10 minutes

Servings: 4

Ingredients:

- 2 eggs
- ¼ cup milk
- ¼ cup ham, diced
- ¼ cup red bell pepper, chopped
- ¼ cup cheddar cheese
- Salt to taste

Method:

1. Beat the eggs in a bowl.
2. Stir in the milk.
3. Add the rest of the ingredients.
4. Pour into a small pan.
5. Add the pan to the air fryer rack.
6. Choose air fry function.
7. Set it to 350 degrees F.
8. Cook for 10 minutes.

Serving Suggestions: Garnish with pepper and chopped green onions.

Preparation & Cooking Tips: Use almond milk if you want your omelette free of dairy.

Sweet Potato Hash

Preparation Time: 10 minutes

Cooking Time: 15 minutes

Servings: 6

Ingredients:

- 2 sweet potatoes, cubed
- 2 slices bacon, diced
- 2 tablespoons olive oil
- 1 tablespoon smoked paprika
- Salt and pepper to taste
- 1 teaspoon dried dill weed

Method:

1. Choose air fry setting.
2. Preheat it to 400 degrees F.
3. In a bowl, combine all the ingredients.
4. Pour into a pan.
5. Place in the air fryer.
6. Cook for 15 minutes, stirring every 3 minutes.

Serving Suggestions: Garnish with chopped parsley.

Preparation & Cooking Tips: You can also use potatoes for this recipe.

Bacon & Eggs

Preparation Time: 10 minutes

Cooking Time: 16 minutes

Servings: 4

Ingredients:

- 8 slices bacon
- 4 sunny side up eggs
- 2 cups avocado, sliced into cubes

Method:

1. Select air fry function.
2. Preheat your air fryer to 390 degrees F.
3. Add the bacon slices to the air fryer rack.
4. Air fry for 8 minutes per side.
5. Serve crispy bacon strips with eggs and avocado.

Serving Suggestions: Garnish with chopped parsley.

Preparation & Cooking Tips: Drain the bacon before serving.

Breakfast Sausage Patties

Preparation Time: 10 minutes

Cooking Time: 10 minutes

Servings: 4

Ingredients:

- Cooking spray
- 12 oz. sausage patties
- 4 slices whole wheat bread

Method:

1. Preheat your air fryer to 400 degrees F.
2. Spray sausage patties with oil.
3. Add the sausage patties to the air fryer rack.
4. Cook for 5 minutes per side.
5. Serve with whole wheat bread slices.

Serving Suggestions: Serve with fresh green salad.

Preparation & Cooking Tips: You can also use turkey sausage patties.

Mexican Hash Browns

Preparation Time: 15 minutes

Cooking Time: 20 minutes

Servings: 4

Ingredients:

- 1 ½ lb. potatoes, cubed
- 1 white onion, diced
- 1 red bell pepper, diced
- 1 jalapeno, sliced into rings
- 2 tablespoons olive oil
- ½ teaspoon ground cumin
- ½ teaspoon taco seasoning mix
- Salt and pepper to taste

Method:

1. Select air fry function in your air fryer.
2. Set it to 320 degrees F.
3. Combine all the ingredients in a bowl.
4. Transfer to a small baking pan.
5. Add to the air fryer.
6. Cook for 20 minutes, stirring once or twice.

Serving Suggestions: Garnish with chopped fresh herbs.

Preparation & Cooking Tips: Be sure to remove the seeds in the peppers.

Breakfast Casserole

Preparation Time: 20 minutes

Cooking Time: 15 minutes

Servings: 4

Ingredients:

- Cooking spray
- 8 eggs, beaten
- ¼ cup white onion, diced
- 1 green bell pepper, diced
- 1 lb. ground sausage, cooked
- ½ cup cheddar cheese, shredded
- Garlic salt to taste

Method:

1. Spray your small baking pan with oil.
2. Combine the ingredients in the baking pan.
3. Place inside the air fryer.
4. Choose air fry setting.
5. Cook at 390 degrees F for 15 minutes.

Serving Suggestions: Sprinkle with ground fennel seed.

Preparation & Cooking Tips: You can also season with salt and pepper instead of garlic salt.

Chapter 3: Chicken Recipes

Orange Chicken

Preparation Time: 20 minutes

Cooking Time: 25 minutes

Servings: 4

Ingredients:

- 1 cup cornstarch
- Salt and pepper to taste
- 1 egg
- ½ lb. chicken breast fillet, sliced into cubes
- 1 teaspoon garlic, grated
- 1 teaspoon ginger, grated
- 1 tablespoon scallions, chopped
- 2 teaspoons brown sugar
- 2 teaspoons reduced-sodium soy sauce
- 1 teaspoon rice vinegar
- 2 tablespoons butter
- 1 cup orange juice
- 1 teaspoon orange zest
- Pinch red pepper flakes

Method:

1. In a bowl, mix the salt, pepper and cornstarch.
2. Beat the egg in another bowl.
3. Dip the chicken cubes in the egg and then coat with the cornstarch mixture.

4. Add the chicken cubes to the air fryer rack.

5. Choose air fry setting.

6. Set it to 400 degrees F.

7. Cook for 15 minutes.

8. In another bowl, mix the remaining ingredients.

9. Add to a baking pan.

10. Stir the chicken into the mixture.

11. Place it back to the air fryer.

12. Choose bake setting.

13. Cook at 350 degrees F for 10 minutes.

Serving Suggestions: Serve with white or brown rice.

Preparation & Cooking Tips: Use freshly squeezed orange juice.

Chicken Reuben

Preparation Time: 10 minutes

Cooking Time: 10 minutes

Servings: 2

Ingredients:

- 2 tablespoons butter
- 4 slice whole wheat bread
- 8 slices Swiss cheese
- 8 strips roasted chicken breast
- 4 tablespoons coleslaw
- 2 tablespoon Russian dressing

Method:

1. Spread the butter on the bread slices.
2. Add the rest of the ingredients on top of the bread slices layer by layer.
3. Top with another bread slice.
4. Place the sandwich inside the air fryer.
5. Choose the bake setting.
6. Set it to 310 degrees F.
7. Cook it for 5 minutes.
8. Flip the sandwich and cook for another 5 minutes.

Serving Suggestions: Slice your sandwiches in half before serving.

Preparation & Cooking Tips: Use unsalted butter.

Chicken Tenders

Preparation Time: 15 minutes

Cooking Time: 15 minutes

Servings: 2

Ingredients:

- ½ cup flour
- 2 eggs
- 1 oz. milk
- 1 cup breadcrumbs
- 4 chicken tenders
- Salt and pepper to taste

Method:

1. Add the flour to a small baking pan.
2. In a bowl, beat the egg and milk.
3. Place the breadcrumbs on a shallow dish.
4. Season chicken with salt and pepper.
5. Coat with the flour.
6. Dip in egg.
7. Dredge with the breadcrumbs.
8. Place inside the air fryer.
9. Choose the air fry setting.
10. Cook at 400 degrees F for 15 minutes, flipping halfway through.

Serving Suggestions: Serve with hot sauce.

Preparation & Cooking Tips: You can make these ahead of time by freezing breaded chicken and air frying when ready to serve.

Chicken Strips with Honey Mustard

Preparation Time: 15 minutes

Cooking Time: 10 minutes

Servings: 4

Ingredients:

Chicken strips

- 1 ½ lb. chicken breast fillet, sliced into strips
- Salt and pepper to taste
- 1 ½ cups all purpose flour
- 2 eggs
- ¼ cup buttermilk
- 2 ½ cups breadcrumbs
- Cooking spray

Honey mustard dip

- 3 tablespoons honey
- 2 tablespoons mustard
- ¼ cup mayonnaise
- Salt and pepper to taste

Method:

1. Sprinkle chicken strips with salt and pepper.
2. Coat with flour.
3. In a bowl, beat eggs and milk.
4. Dip chicken strips in egg mixture.
5. Dredge with breadcrumbs and spray with oil.

6. Arrange in the air fryer rack.

7. Set it to air fry.

8. Cook at 400 degrees F for 5 minutes per side.

9. In a bowl, mix the honey mustard ingredients.

10. Serve chicken with honey mustard sauce.

Serving Suggestions: Serve with green salad.

Preparation & Cooking Tips: Use Dijon style mustard for this recipe.

Chicken Taquitos

Preparation Time: 20 minutes

Cooking Time: 5 minutes

Servings: 12

Ingredients:

- Cooking spray
- 3 cups chicken, cooked and shredded
- 1 chipotle in adobo sauce, minced
- 8 oz. cream cheese
- 1 teaspoon chili powder
- 1 teaspoon cumin
- Salt and pepper to taste
- 1 tsp. cumin
- 1 tsp. chili powder
- 12 corn tortillas
- 2 cups cheddar cheese, shredded

Method:

1. Spray a baking pan with oil.
2. Mix chicken, minced chipotle, cream cheese, chili powder, cumin, salt and pepper.
3. Spread the mixture on top of the tortilla.
4. Top with the cheese.
5. Roll up the tortillas.
6. Add to the air fryer.
7. Choose grill setting.
8. Cook at 400 degrees F for 5 minutes.

Serving Suggestions: Serve with pico de gallo, sour cream and diced avocado.

Preparation & Cooking Tips: Toast the corn tortillas before air frying.

Parmesan Chicken Breast

Preparation Time: 15 minutes

Cooking Time: 16 minutes

Servings: 2

Ingredients:

- ¼ cup all purpose flour
- 1 egg, beaten
- ¾ cup breadcrumbs
- 2 teaspoons lemon zest
- ¼ cup Parmesan cheese, grated
- ½ teaspoon cayenne pepper
- 1 teaspoon dried oregano
- Salt and pepper to taste
- 2 chicken breast fillets

Method:

1. Put the flour in a bowl.
2. Add the egg to another bowl.
3. In a shallow dish, combine the rest of the ingredients except the chicken.
4. Coat the chicken with flour.
5. Dip in egg.
6. Cover with breadcrumb mixture.
7. Add to the air fryer rack.
8. Set it to air fry.
9. Cook at 375 degrees F for 8 minutes per side.

Serving Suggestions: Serve with mayo.

Preparation & Cooking Tips: You can also use chicken thigh fillet for this recipe.

Garlic Parmesan Chicken

Preparation Time: 15 minutes

Cooking Time: 30 minutes

Servings: 4

Ingredients:

- 4 chicken thighs
- Salt and pepper to taste
- 2 eggs, beaten
- 1 cup breadcrumbs
- ¼ cup Parmesan cheese, grated
- 1 teaspoon Italian seasoning
- 1 teaspoon garlic powder

Method:

1. Sprinkle both sides of chicken with the salt and pepper.
2. In a bowl, beat the eggs.
3. Mix the remaining ingredients in another bowl.
4. Dip the chicken in eggs.
5. Cover with the breadcrumb mixture.
6. Air fry at 360 degrees F for 30 minutes, flipping halfway through.

Serving Suggestions: Serve with marinara sauce as dip.

Preparation & Cooking Tips: You can also use garlic salt in place of garlic powder and salt.

Garlic Herb Chicken

Preparation Time: 20 minutes

Cooking Time: 40 minutes

Servings: 6

Ingredients:

- 2 lb. chicken breast fillet
- Salt and pepper to taste
- 3 cloves garlic, minced
- 4 tablespoons butter
- 1 teaspoon thyme, chopped
- 1 teaspoon rosemary, chopped

Method:

1. Season chicken with salt and pepper.
2. In a bowl, mix garlic, butter and herbs.
3. Brush mixture on both sides of chicken.
4. Add to the air fryer.
5. Press the grill setting.
6. Set it to 375 degrees F.
7. Cook for 40 minutes, flipping twice during cooking.

Serving Suggestions: Let rest for 5 to 7 minutes before serving.

Preparation & Cooking Tips: You can also use dried herbs for this recipe.

Spicy Chicken

Preparation Time: 40 minutes

Cooking Time: 20 minutes

Servings: 4

Ingredients:

- 2 teaspoons ginger, grated
- 2 cloves garlic, minced
- ¼ cup olive oil
- ¼ cup soy sauce
- 2 tablespoons chili garlic sauce
- 2 tablespoons honey
- 1 tablespoon lime juice
- 4 chicken thighs

Method:

1. Add all the ingredients except chicken to a bowl.
2. Mix well.
3. Reserve half of the mixture and refrigerate.
4. Stir in chicken thighs in the remaining mixture.
5. Cover and marinate in the refrigerator for 30 minutes.
6. Add the chicken to the air fryer.
7. Set it to grill.
8. Cook at 400 degrees F for 20 minutes, flipping twice.
9. Simmer the reserved sauce in a pan over medium heat.
10. Coat the chicken with the thickened sauce and serve.

Serving Suggestions: Garnish with toasted sesame seeds.

Preparation & Cooking Tips: Use bone-in chicken thighs for this recipe.

Chapter 4: Beef Recipes

Garlic Butter Steak with Herbs

Preparation Time: 15 minutes

Cooking Time: 15 minutes

Servings: 2

Ingredients:

- 2 cloves garlic, minced
- 4 tablespoons butter
- 1 teaspoon chives, chopped
- 2 teaspoons parsley, chopped
- 1 teaspoon rosemary, chopped
- 1 teaspoon thyme, chopped
- 2 rib eye steaks
- Salt and pepper to taste

Method:

1. Combine the garlic, butter and herbs in a bowl.
2. Refrigerate for 20 minutes.
3. Roll the butter mixture into a log.
4. Sprinkle both sides of steaks with salt and pepper.
5. Set air fryer to grill.
6. Air fry at 400 degrees F for 15 minutes, flipping once or twice.
7. Slice the herb butter.
8. Top the steaks with the herb butter.

Serving Suggestions: Let steak rest for 10 minutes before serving.

Preparation & Cooking Tips: You can also use t-bone steak for this recipe.

Cheeseburger

Preparation Time: 20 minutes

Cooking Time: 16 minutes

Servings: 4

Ingredients:

- 1 lb. ground beef
- 1 tablespoon soy sauce
- 2 cloves garlic, minced
- Salt and pepper to taste
- 4 slices American cheese
- 4 burger buns, split
- 4 tablespoons mayonnaise
- 2 cups lettuce leaves
- 1 red onion, sliced thinly
- 1 tomato, sliced

Method:

1. Mix the ground beef, soy sauce and garlic.
2. Sprinkle with salt and pepper.
3. Add the patties to the air fryer.
4. Set it to grill.
5. Cook at 375 degrees F for 8 minutes per side.
6. Spread bottom burger buns with mayo.
7. Top with the patties, lettuce, onion and tomato.
8. Add buns on top.

Serving Suggestions: Toast the burger before serving.

Preparation & Cooking Tips: Use lean ground beef for this recipe.

Beef Mac & Cheese

Preparation Time: 30 minutes

Cooking Time: 35 minutes

Servings: 4

Ingredients:

- ½ lb. elbow macaroni
- 1 cup chicken broth
- 2 cups milk
- 8 oz. cheddar cheese, shredded
- 4 tablespoons cream cheese
- 4 tablespoons butter
- 1 cup ground beef, cooked
- Salt and pepper to taste
- 1 teaspoon dry mustard
- Pinch cayenne pepper
- Nutmeg, grated
- 1 cup mozzarella cheese, shredded

Method:

1. In a pot filled with water, cook the pasta according to package directions.
2. Drain and set aside.
3. In a pan over medium heat, mix the broth, milk, cheese, cream cheese and butter.
4. Simmer for 5 minutes.
5. Pour broth mixture into a baking pan.
6. Stir in the pasta and the rest of the ingredients except the mozzarella cheese.
7. Top with the mozzarella cheese.

8. Cover with foil.

9. Choose bake setting.

10. Cook at 400 degrees F for 30 minutes.

Serving Suggestions: Garnish with chopped parsley.

Preparation & Cooking Tips: Use lean ground beef for this recipe.

Steak with Mashed Cauliflower

Preparation Time: 15 minutes

Cooking Time: 12 minutes

Servings: 2

Ingredients:

- 2 rib eye steaks
- Salt and pepper to taste
- 2 tablespoons butter
- 2 cups cauliflower florets, roasted
- ¼ cup almond milk

Method:

1. Choose grill setting in your air fryer.
2. Set it to 400 degrees F.
3. Sprinkle both sides of steak with salt and pepper.
4. Add the steaks to the air fryer.
5. Cook for 12 minutes, flipping halfway through.
6. Add cauliflower florets to a food processor.
7. Stir in almond milk, salt and pepper.
8. Pulse until smooth.
9. Serve steaks with mashed cauliflower.

Serving Suggestions: Extend cooking to 15 minutes for well-done steak.

Preparation & Cooking Tips: You can also use New York strip steaks for this recipe.

Beef & Asparagus

Preparation Time: 40 minutes

Cooking Time: 10 minutes

Servings: 2

Ingredients:

- 2 New York strips steaks, sliced into cubes

Marinade

- 1 teaspoon olive oil
- 1 teaspoon steak seasoning
- ½ teaspoon dried onion powder
- ½ teaspoon dried garlic powder
- Salt and pepper to taste
- Pinch cayenne pepper

Asparagus

- 1 lb. asparagus
- Salt to taste
- 1 teaspoon olive oil

Method:

1. Preheat your air fryer to 400 degrees F.
2. Combine marinade ingredients in a bowl.
3. Stir in steak cubes.
4. Cover and marinate for 30 minutes.
5. Air fry at 5 minutes.

6.   Coat asparagus with oil.

7.   Season with salt.

8.   Add asparagus to the air fryer.

9.   Toss to combine.

10. Cook for another 3 to 5 minutes.

Serving Suggestions: Garnish with chopped parsley.

Preparation & Cooking Tips: You can also use beef chuck for this recipe.

Country Steak

Preparation Time: 15 minutes

Cooking Time: 20 minutes

Servings: 2

Ingredients:

- ¼ cup cornstarch
- ½ cup flour
- 1 teaspoon paprika
- 1 teaspoon onion powder
- 1 teaspoon garlic powder
- 2 rib eye steaks
- Salt and pepper to taste
- 1 egg, beaten
- Cooking spray

Method:

1. Combine cornstarch, flour, paprika, onion powder and garlic powder in a bowl.
2. Season steaks with salt and pepper.
3. Coat steaks with egg.
4. Dredge with cornstarch mixture.
5. Spray with oil.
6. Choose bake setting in the air fryer.
7. Cook at 400 degrees F for 8 to 10 minutes per side or until golden.

Serving Suggestions: Serve with roasted potatoes and gravy.

Preparation & Cooking Tips: Add cayenne pepper if you want your steak spicy.

Beef & Green Beans

Preparation Time: 15 minutes

Cooking Time: 25 minutes

Servings: 4

Ingredients:

Beef and green beans

- 1 lb. flank steak, sliced thinly
- ¼ cup cornstarch
- 1 lb. green beans, trimmed, sliced and steamed

Sauce

- 2 teaspoons vegetable oil
- ½ teaspoon ginger
- 1 tablespoon garlic, minced
- ½ cup soy sauce
- ½ cup water
- ¾ cup brown sugar

Method:

1. Coat steak strips with cornstarch.
2. Select air fry setting.
3. Cook at 390 degrees F for 5 to 7 minutes per side.
4. Add sauce ingredients to a pan over medium heat.
5. Simmer for 10 minutes.
6. Dip the steaks in sauce.
7. Serve with green beans.

Serving Suggestions: Serve with hot rice.

Preparation & Cooking Tips: You can also use steamed carrots in place of green beans.

Roast Beef

Preparation Time: 10 minutes

Cooking Time: 30 minutes

Servings: 6

Ingredients:

- 4 lb. beef roast
- 1 tablespoon olive oil
- 1 teaspoon steak seasoning

Method:

1. Drizzle roast with oil.
2. Sprinkle with steak seasoning.
3. Add to the air fryer.
4. Select rotisserie.
5. Cook at 360 degrees F for 50 minutes.

Serving Suggestions: Let rest for 5 minutes before serving.

Preparation & Cooking Tips: For well-done, final internal temperature should be 160 degrees F.

Burger Steak

Preparation Time: 20 minutes

Cooking Time: 20 minutes

Servings: 2

Ingredients:

- 1 lb. ground beef
- 1 tablespoon parsley, chopped
- 1 onion, minced
- Salt and pepper to taste
- 1 cup mushroom gravy

Method:

1. Mix ground beef, parsley, onion, salt and pepper in a bowl.
2. Form patties from the mixture.
3. Choose grill setting in the air fryer.
4. Set it to 375 degrees F.
5. Cook the burgers for 8 to 10 minutes per side.
6. Pour mushroom gravy on top and serve.

Serving Suggestions: Serve with fresh green salad.

Preparation & Cooking Tips: You can also combine ½ lb. ground beef and ½ lb. ground pork.

Chapter 5: Pork Recipes

Spring Rolls

Preparation Time: 15 minutes

Cooking Time: 8 minutes

Servings: 4

Ingredients:

- 8 rice paper wrappers
- 4 cups ground pork, cooked
- 2 cloves garlic, minced
- 3 scallions, chopped
- 1 tablespoon ginger, minced
- 2 cup shiitake mushrooms
- 1 cup carrot, sliced into thin strips
- 1 teaspoon sesame oil
- 3 tablespoons soy sauce
- 2 tablespoons cilantro

Method:

1. Add rice paper wrappers on your kitchen table.
2. Mix the remaining ingredients in a bowl.
3. Top each of the wrappers with the ground pork mixture.
4. Roll up the wrappers.
5. Place in the air fryer.
6. Choose air fry setting.
7. Cook at 400 degrees F for 5 minutes.

8. Turn and cook for another 3 minutes.

Serving Suggestions: Serve with chili dipping sauce.

Preparation & Cooking Tips: Use lean ground pork.

Parmesan Pork Chops

Preparation Time: 10 minutes

Cooking Time: 15 minutes

Servings: 4

Ingredients:

- 4 pork chops
- 2 tablespoons olive oil
- 1 teaspoon onion powder
- 1 teaspoon garlic powder
- 1 teaspoon paprika
- ½ cup Parmesan cheese, grated
- Salt and pepper to taste

Method:

1. Brush pork chops with oil.
2. In a bowl, mix the remaining ingredients.
3. Sprinkle pork chops with spice mixture.
4. Add to the air fryer.
5. Choose grill setting.
6. Cook at 375 degrees F for 5 to 7 minutes per side.

Serving Suggestions: Serve with marinara dipping sauce.

Preparation & Cooking Tips: Use bone-in pork chops for this recipe.

Bacon & Broccoli Rice Bowl

Preparation Time: 10 minutes

Cooking Time: 10 minutes

Servings: 4

Ingredients:

- 8 slices bacon
- 4 cups cooked rice
- 4 cups broccoli, steamed
- 1 carrot, sliced into thin sticks

Method:

1. Add the bacon to the air fryer.
2. Set it to air fry.
3. Cook at 400 degrees F for 10 minutes or until crispy.
4. Add rice to serving bowls.
5. Top with the bacon, broccoli and carrots.

Serving Suggestions: Drizzle with hot sauce.

Preparation & Cooking Tips: You can also roast broccoli in the air fryer if you like.

Paprika Pork Chops with Corn

Preparation Time: 10 minutes

Cooking Time: 15 minutes

Servings: 4

Ingredients:

- 4 boneless pork chops
- 2 tablespoons olive oil
- 2 teaspoons paprika
- 1 teaspoon onion powder
- Salt and pepper to taste
- 4 ears corn, grilled

Method:

1. Brush both sides of pork chops with oil.
2. Season with paprika, onion powder, salt and pepper.
3. Add pork chops to the air fryer.
4. Set it to grill.
5. Cook at 375 degrees F for 5 to 7 minutes per side.
6. Serve with grilled corn.

Serving Suggestions: Serve with mustard.

Preparation & Cooking Tips: Use boneless pork chops.

Barbecue Pork Tenderloin

Preparation Time: 10 minutes

Cooking Time: 20 minutes

Servings: 2

Ingredients:

- ½ lb. pork tenderloin, diced
- ¼ cup barbecue sauce
- 1 teaspoon olive oil

Method:

1. Coat the pork tenderloin in olive oil.
2. Brush with barbecue sauce.
3. Place in the air fryer rack.
4. Choose grill function.
5. Cook at 375 degrees F for 15 to 20 minutes.

Serving Suggestions: Serve with vinegar dipping sauce.

Preparation & Cooking Tips: Use lean pork tenderloin.

Garlic Pork Chops with Roasted Broccoli

Preparation Time: 10 minutes

Cooking Time: 10 minutes

Servings: 2

Ingredients:

- 2 pork chops
- 2 tablespoons avocado oil, divided
- 1 teaspoon garlic powder
- ½ teaspoon paprika
- Salt to taste
- 2 cups broccoli florets
- 2 cloves garlic, minced

Method:

1. Preheat your air fryer to 350 degrees F.
2. Choose air fry setting.
3. Drizzle pork chops with half of avocado oil.
4. Season with garlic powder, paprika and salt.
5. Add to the air fryer.
6. Cook for 5 minutes.
7. Toss the broccoli in remaining oil.
8. Sprinkle with minced garlic and salt.
9. Add broccoli to the air fryer.
10. Cook for another 5 minutes.

Serving Suggestions: Drizzle with hot sauce and serve.

Preparation & Cooking Tips: Use pork chops that are ½ inch thick.

Pork Belly Bites

Preparation Time: 15 minutes

Cooking Time: 20 minutes

Servings: 4

Ingredients:

- 1 lb. pork belly, diced
- Salt and pepper to taste
- ½ teaspoon garlic powder
- 1 teaspoon Worcestershire sauce

Method:

1. Select the grill setting in your air fryer.
2. Preheat it to 400 degrees F.
3. Season pork with salt, pepper, garlic powder and Worcestershire sauce.
4. Add to the air fryer.
5. Cook at 400 degrees F for 20 minutes, flipping twice.

Serving Suggestions: Serve with barbecue sauce.

Preparation & Cooking Tips: Add cayenne pepper if you like your pork belly bites spicy.

Mustard Herbed Pork Chops

Preparation Time: 40 minutes

Cooking Time: 20 minutes

Servings: 4

Ingredients:

- 2 teaspoons Dijon mustard
- 4 teaspoons white wine
- 4 teaspoons olive oil
- 4 pork chops
- 1 teaspoon dried rosemary leaves
- 1 teaspoon ground coriander
- 1 clove garlic, minced
- Salt and pepper to taste

Method:

1. Mix mustard, wine and oil in a bowl.
2. Add pork chops and marinate for 30 minutes.
3. Sprinkle with rosemary, coriander, garlic, salt and pepper.
4. Choose grill setting in the air fryer.
5. Preheat it to 350 degrees F.
6. Add pork chops to the air fryer.
7. Cook for 10 minutes per side.

Serving Suggestions: Let pork chops rest for 5 minutes before serving.

Preparation & Cooking Tips: Use pork chops that are ¾ inch thick.

Pork Chops with Creamy Dip

Preparation Time: 10 minutes

Cooking Time: 30 minutes

Servings: 4

Ingredients:

Sauce

- 3 tablespoons mayonnaise
- 1 teaspoon apple cider vinegar
- 1 tablespoon honey
- 1 tablespoon mustard
- ¼ teaspoon paprika
- Salt and pepper to taste

Pork

- 4 pork chops
- Salt and pepper to taste
- ¼ cup all-purpose flour
- 2 eggs
- ¾ cup breadcrumbs

Method:

1. In a bowl, mix the ingredients for sauce.
2. Refrigerate until serving time.
3. Season pork chops with salt and pepper.
4. Coat with flour.
5. Dip in eggs and dredge with breadcrumbs.

6. Press air fry setting.

7. Cook at 360 degrees F for 30 minutes, flipping once.

8. Serve pork chops with dip.

Serving Suggestions: Serve with fresh green salad.

Preparation & Cooking Tips: Use Dijon mustard.

Chapter 6: Fish & Seafood Recipes

Shrimp Bang Bang

Preparation Time: 10 minutes

Cooking Time: 4 minutes

Servings: 4

Ingredients:

- 1 cup cornstarch
- ¼ teaspoon Sriracha powder
- 2 lb. shrimp, peeled and deveined
- ¼ cup mayonnaise
- ¼ cup sweet chili sauce

Method:

1. In a bowl, combine cornstarch and Sriracha powder.
2. Dredge shrimp with this mixture.
3. Place shrimp in the air fryer.
4. Choose air fry setting.
5. Cook at 400 degrees F for 7 minutes per side.
6. Mix the mayo and chili sauce.
7. Serve shrimp with sauce.

Serving Suggestions: Serve on top of lettuce leaves.

Preparation & Cooking Tips: You can also use peeled frozen shrimp for this recipe.

Honey Glazed Salmon

Preparation Time: 15 minutes

Cooking Time: 30 minutes

Servings: 1

Ingredients:

- ¼ cup soy sauce
- ½ cup honey
- 1 tablespoon lemon juice
- 1 oz. orange juice
- 1 tablespoon brown sugar
- 1 teaspoon olive oil
- 1 tablespoon red wine vinegar
- 1 scallion, chopped
- 1 clove garlic, minced
- Salt and pepper to taste
- 1 salmon fillet

Method:

1. Mix all the ingredients except salt, pepper and salmon.
2. Place mixture in a pan over medium heat.
3. Bring to a boil.
4. Reduce heat.
5. Simmer for 15 minutes.
6. Turn off heat and transfer sauce to a bowl.
7. Sprinkle salt and pepper on both sides of salmon.
8. Add salmon to the air fryer.

9. Select grill function.

10. Cook at 320 degrees F for 6 minutes per side.

11. Brush with the sauce.

12. Cook for another 5 minutes per side.

13. Serve with remaining sauce.

Serving Suggestions: Garnish with chopped scallions.

Preparation & Cooking Tips: Simply double the portions to make this dinner for 2.

Salmon with Thyme & Mustard

Preparation Time: 10 minutes

Cooking Time: 10 minutes

Servings: 2

Ingredients:

- 2 salmon fillets
- Salt and pepper to taste
- ½ teaspoon dried thyme
- 2 tablespoons mustard
- 2 teaspoons olive oil
- 1 clove garlic, minced
- 1 tablespoon brown sugar

Method:

1. Sprinkle salt and pepper on both sides of salmon.
2. In a bowl, combine the remaining ingredients.
3. Spread this mixture on top of the salmon.
4. Place the salmon in the air fryer.
5. Choose air fry function.
6. Cook at 400 degrees F for 10 minutes.

Serving Suggestions: Garnish with chopped fresh herbs.

Preparation & Cooking Tips: Use whole grain mustard.

Crispy Fish Fillet

Preparation Time: 15 minutes

Cooking Time: 12 minutes

Servings: 2

Ingredients:

- 2 cod fillets
- 1 teaspoon Old Bay seasoning
- Salt and pepper to taste
- ½ cup all-purpose flour
- 1 egg, beaten
- 2 cups breadcrumbs

Method:

1. Sprinkle both sides of cod with Old Bay seasoning, salt and pepper.
2. Coat with flour, dip in egg and dredge with breadcrumbs.
3. Add fish to the air fryer.
4. Select air fry setting.
5. Cook at 400 degrees F for 5 to 6 minutes per side.

Serving Suggestions: Garnish with lemon wedges.

Preparation & Cooking Tips: You can also use a different type of white fish fillet for this recipe.

Garlic Butter Lobster Tails

Preparation Time: 15 minutes

Cooking Time: 8 minutes

Servings: 2

Ingredients:

- 2 lobster tails
- 2 cloves garlic, minced
- 2 tablespoons butter
- 1 teaspoon lemon juice
- 1 teaspoon chopped chives
- Salt to taste

Method:

1. Butterfly the lobster tails.
2. Place the meat on top of the shell.
3. Mix the remaining ingredients in a bowl.
4. Add lobster tails inside the air fryer.
5. Set it to air fry.
6. Spread garlic butter on the meat.
7. Cook at 380 degrees F for 5 minutes.
8. Spread more butter on top.
9. Cook for another 2 to 3 minutes.

Serving Suggestions: Garnish with chopped chives.

Preparation & Cooking Tips: You can use frozen lobster tails for this recipe but extend cooking time to 12 minutes.

Pesto Fish

Preparation Time: 15 minutes

Cooking Time: 10 minutes

Servings: 4

Ingredients:

- 1 tablespoon olive oil
- 4 fish fillets
- Salt and pepper to taste
- 1 cup olive oil
- 3 cloves garlic
- 1 ½ cups fresh basil leaves
- 2 tablespoons Parmesan cheese, grated
- 3 tablespoons pine nuts

Method:

1. Drizzle olive oil over fish fillets and season with salt and pepper.
2. Add remaining ingredients to a food processor.
3. Pulse until smooth.
4. Transfer pesto to a bowl and set aside.
5. Add fish to the air fryer.
6. Select grill setting.
7. Cook at 320 degrees F for 5 minutes per side.
8. Spread pesto on top of the fish before serving.

Serving Suggestions: Sprinkle with chopped pine nuts.

Preparation & Cooking Tips: Use cod or any white fish fillet for this recipe.

Lemon Garlic Fish Fillet

Preparation Time: 10 minutes

Cooking Time: 20 minutes

Servings: 2

Ingredients:

- 2 white fish fillets
- Cooking spray
- ½ teaspoon lemon pepper
- ½ teaspoon garlic powder
- Salt and pepper to taste
- 2 teaspoon lemon juice

Method:

1. Choose bake setting in your air fryer oven.
2. Preheat it to 360 degrees F.
3. Spray fish fillets with oil.
4. Season fish fillets with lemon pepper, garlic powder, salt and pepper.
5. Add to the air fryer.
6. Cook at 360 degrees F for 20 minutes.
7. Drizzle with lemon juice.

Serving Suggestions: Garnish with lemon slices.

Preparation & Cooking Tips: Use tilapia or cod fillet for this recipe.

Blackened Tilapia

Preparation Time: 10 minutes

Cooking Time: 10 minutes

Servings: 4

Ingredients:

- 4 tilapia fillets
- Cooking spray
- 2 teaspoons brown sugar
- 2 tablespoons paprika
- ¼ teaspoon cayenne pepper
- 1 teaspoon garlic powder
- 1 teaspoon dried oregano
- ½ teaspoon cumin
- Salt to taste

Method:

1. Spray fish fillets with oil.
2. Mix the remaining ingredients in a bowl.
3. Sprinkle both sides of fish with spice mixture.
4. Add to the air fryer.
5. Set it to air fry.
6. Cook at 400 degrees F for 4 to 5 minutes per side.

Serving Suggestions: Serve with fresh green salad.

Preparation & Cooking Tips: You can also use other types of white fish fillet for this recipe.

Fish & Sweet Potato Chips

Preparation Time: 20 minutes

Cooking Time: 25 minutes

Servings: 2

Ingredients:

- 4 cups sweet potatoes, sliced into strips
- 1 teaspoon olive oil
- 1 egg, beaten
- 2/3 cup breadcrumbs
- 1 teaspoon lemon zest
- 2 fish fillets, sliced into strips
- ½ cup Greek yogurt
- 1 tablespoon shallots, chopped
- 1 tablespoon chives, chopped
- 2 teaspoons dill, chopped

Method:

1. Toss sweet potatoes in oil.
2. Cook in the air fryer at 360 degrees F for 10 minutes or until crispy.
3. Set aside.
4. Dip fish fillet in egg.
5. Dredge with breadcrumbs mixed with lemon zest.
6. Air fry at 360 degrees F for 12 minutes.
7. Mix yogurt and remaining ingredients.
8. Serve fish, sweet potato chips and sauce together.

Serving Suggestions: Garnish with chopped parsley.

Preparation & Cooking Tips: Use panko breadcrumbs for this recipe.

Chapter 7: Vegetarian Recipes

Tofu Nuggets

Preparation Time: 15 minutes

Cooking Time: 25 minutes

Servings: 4

Ingredients:

Tofu

- 14 oz. tofu, sliced into cubes
- Cooking spray
- ¼ cup flour
- 1 teaspoon garlic powder
- ½ teaspoon paprika
- ½ teaspoon ground cumin
- Salt to taste

Sauce

- 1 tablespoon avocado oil
- 2 tablespoons sugar
- 3 tablespoons soy sauce
- 2 tablespoons honey
- 1 teaspoon garlic powder
- 1 tablespoon ginger, grated
- Pepper to taste

Method:

1. Spray tofu cubes with oil.

2. Mix remaining ingredients in a bowl.

3. Coat tofu evenly with this mixture.

4. Add the tofu cubes to the air fryer.

5. Set it to air fry.

6. Cook at 350 degrees F for 10 minutes.

7. Toss and cook for 15 minutes.

8. In a bowl, mix the sauce ingredients.

9. Toss the tofu in the sauce and serve.

Serving Suggestions: Garnish with sesame seeds and chopped chives.

Preparation & Cooking Tips: Use maple syrup if honey is not available.

Zucchini Lasagna

Preparation Time: 15 minutes

Cooking Time: 15 minutes

Servings: 4

Ingredients:

- 1 zucchini, sliced thinly lengthwise and divided
- ½ cup marinara sauce, divided
- ¼ cup ricotta, divided
- 1 cup fresh basil leaves, chopped and divided
- ¼ cup spinach leaves, chopped and divided

Method:

1. Layer half of the zucchini slices in a small loaf pan.
2. Spread with half of marinara sauce and ricotta.
3. Top with half of spinach and basil.
4. Repeat layers with the remaining ingredients.
5. Cover the pan with foil.
6. Place inside the air fryer.
7. Set it to bake.
8. Cook at 400 degrees F for 10 minutes.
9. Remove foil and cook for another 5 minutes.

Serving Suggestions: Garnish with fresh basil.

Preparation & Cooking Tips: Make this ahead of time by freezing and baking when ready to serve.

Veggie Rolls

Preparation Time: 20 minutes

Cooking Time: 20 minutes

Servings: 5

Ingredients:

- 1 tablespoon olive oil
- 1 clove garlic, minced
- 1 teaspoon ginger, minced
- 3 scallions, chopped
- ½ lb. mushrooms, chopped
- 2 cups cabbage, chopped
- 8 oz. water chestnuts, diced
- Salt and pepper to taste
- 6 spring roll wrappers
- 1 tablespoon water

Method:

1. Add oil to a pan over medium heat.
2. Cook the garlic, ginger, scallions and mushrooms for 2 minutes.
3. Stir in the remaining vegetables.
4. Season with salt and pepper.
5. Cook for 3 minutes, stirring.
6. Transfer to a strainer.
7. Add vegetables on top of the wrappers.
8. Roll up the wrappers.
9. Seal the edges with water.

10. Place the rolls inside the air fryer.

11. Choose air fry setting.

12. Cook at 360 degrees F for 15 minutes.

Serving Suggestions: Serve with vinegar dipping sauce.

Preparation & Cooking Tips: Cook in batches.

Onion Rings

Preparation Time: 10 minutes

Cooking Time: 10 minutes

Servings: 3

Ingredients:

- 2 white onions, sliced into rings
- 1 cup flour
- 2 eggs, beaten
- 1 cup breadcrumbs

Method:

1. Cover the onion rings with flour.
2. Dip in the egg.
3. Dredge with breadcrumbs.
4. Add to the air fryer.
5. Set it to air fry.
6. Cook at 400 degrees F for 10 minutes.

Serving Suggestions: Serve with tartar sauce.

Preparation & Cooking Tips: Make ahead of time and freeze. Air fry when ready to serve.

Cheesy Egg Rolls

Preparation Time: 15 minutes

Cooking Time: 12 minutes

Servings: 12

Ingredients:

- 12 spring roll wrappers
- 12 slices provolone cheese
- 3 eggs, cooked and sliced
- 1 carrot, sliced into thin strips
- 1 tablespoon water

Method:

1. Top the wrappers with cheese, eggs and carrot strips.
2. Roll up the wrappers and seal with water.
3. Place inside the air fryer.
4. Set it to air fry.
5. Cook at 390 degrees F for 12 minutes, turning once or twice.

Serving Suggestions: Serve with ketchup or sweet chili sauce.

Preparation & Cooking Tips: You can also use cheddar cheese for this recipe.

Cauliflower Bites

Preparation Time: 15 minutes

Cooking Time: 10 minutes

Servings: 6

Ingredients:

Cauliflower bites

- 4 cups cauliflower rice
- 1 egg, beaten
- 1 cup Parmesan cheese, grated
- 1 cup cheddar, shredded
- 2 tablespoons chives, chopped
- ¼ cup breadcrumbs
- Salt and pepper to taste

Sauce

- ½ cup ketchup
- 2 tablespoons hot sauce

Method:

1. Combine cauliflower bites ingredients in a bowl.
2. Mix well.
3. Form balls from the mixture.
4. Choose air fry setting.
5. Add cauliflower bites to the air fryer.
6. Cook at 375 degrees F for 10 minutes.
7. Mix ketchup and hot sauce.

8.   Serve cauliflower bites with dip.

Serving Suggestions: Garnish with chopped parsley.

Preparation & Cooking Tips: You can make your own cauliflower rice by pulsing cauliflower florets in a food processor.

Baked Potatoes

Preparation Time: 20 minutes

Cooking Time: 45 minutes

Servings: 6

Ingredients:

- 6 potatoes
- 1 tablespoon olive oil
- Salt to taste
- 1 cup butter
- ½ cup milk
- ½ cup sour cream
- 1 ½ cup cheddar, shredded and divided

Method:

1. Poke the potatoes using a fork.
2. Add to the air fryer.
3. Set it to bake.
4. Cook at 400 degrees F for 40 minutes.
5. Take out of the oven.
6. Slice the potato in half
7. Scoop out the potato flesh.
8. Mix potato flesh with the remaining ingredients.
9. Put the mixture back to the potato shells.
10. Bake in the air fryer for 5 minutes.

Serving Suggestions: Garnish with chopped green onions.

Preparation & Cooking Tips: Use large Russet potatoes.

Vegetarian Pizza

Preparation Time: 15 minutes

Cooking Time: 10 minutes

Servings: 1

Ingredients:

- 1 pizza crust
- 1 tablespoon olive oil
- ¼ cup tomato sauce
- 1 cup mushrooms
- ½ cup black olives, sliced
- 1 clove garlic, minced
- ½ teaspoon oregano
- Salt and pepper to taste
- 1 cup mozzarella, shredded

Method:

1. Brush pizza crust with oil.
2. Spread tomato sauce on top.
3. Arrange mushrooms and olives on top.
4. Sprinkle with garlic and oregano.
5. Season with salt and pepper.
6. Top with mozzarella cheese.
7. Place inside the air fryer.
8. Set it to bake.
9. Cook at 400 degrees F for 10 minutes.

Serving Suggestions: Garnish with fresh basil leaves.

Preparation & Cooking Tips: Use 8-inch diameter pizza crust.

Brussels Sprout Chips

Preparation Time: 10 minutes

Cooking Time: 15 minutes

Servings: 2

Ingredients:

- 2 cups Brussels sprouts, sliced thinly
- 1 tablespoon olive oil
- 1 teaspoon garlic powder
- Salt and pepper to taste
- 2 tablespoons Parmesan cheese, grated

Method:

1. Toss the Brussels sprouts in oil.
2. Sprinkle with garlic powder, salt, pepper and Parmesan cheese.
3. Choose bake function.
4. Add the Brussels sprouts in the air fryer.
5. Cook at 350 degrees F for 8 minutes.
6. Flip and cook for 7 more minutes.

Serving Suggestions: Serve with Caesar dressing for dipping.

Preparation & Cooking Tips: You can also use this recipe for other vegetables like cauliflower or broccoli.

Chapter 8: Appetizer & Snack Recipes

Pumpkin Seeds

Preparation Time: 5 minutes

Cooking Time: 25 minutes

Servings: 6

Ingredients:

- 2 cups pumpkin seeds
- Water
- 1 ½ tablespoons butter
- ½ teaspoon garlic salt

Method:

1. Add pumpkin seeds to a pot filled with water.
2. Bring to a boil
3. Drain the seeds.
4. Let cool for 5 minutes.
5. Toss pumpkin seeds in butter.
6. Season with garlic salt.
7. Add to the air fryer.
8. Set it to air fry.
9. Cook at 360 degrees F for 15 minutes, shaking once.

Serving Suggestions: Adjust seasonings before serving.

Preparation & Cooking Tips: Store in an airtight jar for up to 1 week.

Roasted Garlic Dip

Preparation Time: 10 minutes

Cooking Time: 20 minutes

Servings: 6

Ingredients:

- 1 head garlic
- ½ tablespoon olive oil

Method:

1. Slice the top off the garlic.
2. Drizzle with the olive oil.
3. Add to the air fryer.
4. Set it to roast.
5. Cook at 390 degrees F for 20 minutes.
6. Peel the garlic.
7. Transfer to a food processor.
8. Pulse until smooth.

Serving Suggestions: Serve with chips or crackers.

Preparation & Cooking Tips: Store in an airtight jar for up to 3 days.

Bacon Onion Rings

Preparation Time: 15 minutes

Cooking Time: 10 minutes

Servings: 4

Ingredients:

- 2 white onions, sliced into rings
- 1 tablespoon hot sauce
- 10 bacon slices

Method:

1. Coat onion rings with hot sauce.
2. Wrap each onion ring with bacon.
3. Add to the air fryer.
4. Set it to air fry.
5. Cook at 370 degrees F for 5 minutes per side.

Serving Suggestions: Serve with mayo and ketchup.

Preparation & Cooking Tips: You can also brush onion rings with olive oil instead of hot sauce.

Grilled Cheese Sandwich

Preparation Time: 5 minutes

Cooking Time: 8 minutes

Servings: 1

Ingredients:

- 2 slices bread
- 1 tablespoon butter
- 2 slices cheddar cheese

Method:

1. Spread one side of bread slices with butter.
2. Place the cheese between the two bread slices.
3. Choose grill setting in your air fryer.
4. Cook at 350 degrees F for 5 minutes.
5. Flip and cook for another 3 minutes.

Serving Suggestions: Serve with fresh green salad.

Preparation & Cooking Tips: Use whole wheat bread.

Avocado Fries with Bacon

Preparation Time: 10 minutes

Cooking Time: 10 minutes

Servings: 6

Ingredients:

- 1 avocado, sliced into wedges
- 12 to 15 strips bacon
- Cooking spray

Method:

1. Wrap the avocado wedges with bacon.
2. Spray with oil.
3. Add to the air fryer.
4. Set it to air fry.
5. Cook at 400 degrees F for 10 minutes.

Serving Suggestions: Serve with ranch dressing for dipping.

Preparation & Cooking Tips: For lower-calorie appetizer, use turkey bacon instead.

Beef Empanada

Preparation Time: 20 minutes

Cooking Time: 20 minutes

Servings: 2

Ingredients:

- 1 tablespoon olive oil
- ½ lb. ground beef
- ½ onion, minced
- 1 clove garlic, minced
- 1 green bell pepper, diced
- ¼ cup tomato salsa
- Salt and pepper to taste
- ¼ teaspoon cumin
- 1 egg yolk
- 1 tablespoon milk
- 1 pack empanada shells

Method:

1. Add oil to a pan over medium heat.
2. Cook the ground beef for 5 minutes.
3. Drain the fat.
4. Stir in the onion and garlic.
5. Cook for 4 minutes.
6. Add bell pepper and salsa.
7. Season with salt, pepper and cumin.
8. Cook for 10 minutes.

9. In a bowl, mix egg yolk and milk.

10. Place ground beef mixture on top of the empanada shells.

11. Fold and seal.

12. Brush both sides with egg wash.

13. Add empanada to the air fryer.

14. Set it to air fry.

15. Cook at 400 degrees F for 10 minutes.

Serving Suggestions: Serve with coffee.

Preparation & Cooking Tips: Use lean ground beef.

Potato Tots

Preparation Time: 5 minutes

Cooking Time: 8 minutes

Servings: 4

Ingredients:

- 12 potato tots
- 12 bacon strips

Method:

1. Wrap the potato tots with bacon strips.
2. Add to the air fryer.
3. Set it to air fry.
4. Cook at 400 degrees F for 8 minutes, turning once or twice.

Serving Suggestions: Serve with sour cream dip.

Preparation & Cooking Tips: Use turkey bacon instead of pork to reduce calorie and fat intake.

Coconut Shrimp

Preparation Time: 10 minutes

Cooking Time: 6 minutes

Servings: 3

Ingredients:

- 9 shrimp, peeled and deveined
- ½ cup flour
- 1 egg
- 1 cup breadcrumbs
- 1 cup coconut flakes

Method:

1. Coat shrimp with flour.
2. Dip in egg.
3. Dredge with a mixture of breadcrumbs and coconut flakes.
4. Arrange shrimp in the air fryer.
5. Set it to air fry.
6. Cook at 320 degrees F for 6 minutes per side.

Serving Suggestions: Serve with mayo and hot sauce.

Preparation & Cooking Tips: You can also use frozen shrimp recipe but extend cooking time to 15 minutes.

Garlic Knots

Preparation Time: 10 minutes

Cooking Time: 15 minutes

Servings: 2

Ingredients:

- 1 pizza dough
- ½ cup olive oil
- 5 cloves garlic, minced
- Salt to taste
- ¼ cup parsley, chopped
- ¼ cup Parmesan cheese, grated

Method:

1. Divide pizza dough into 2.
2. Roll into a rope.
3. Make a knot with the dough.
4. Mix the remaining ingredients in a bowl.
5. Brush the top with this mixture.
6. Place these inside the air fryer.
7. Set it to bake.
8. Cook at 360 degrees F for 15 minutes, flipping halfway through.

Serving Suggestions: Serve with marinara sauce.

Preparation & Cooking Tips: You can also use garlic powder in place of minced garlic.

Chapter 9: Dessert Recipes

Choco Hazelnut Croissant

Preparation Time: 15 minutes

Cooking Time: 10 minutes

Servings: 2

Ingredients:

- 1 oz. canned crescent rolls
- 8 teaspoons chocolate hazelnut spread

Method:

1. Separate crescent dough into triangles.
2. Spread top with chocolate hazelnut spread.
3. Roll up the triangles to form a crescent shape.
4. Place these in the air fryer.
5. Select bake setting.
6. Cook at 320 degrees F for 8 to 10 minutes or until golden.

Serving Suggestions: Drizzle with melted chocolate on top before serving.

Preparation & Cooking Tips: You can also add chopped almonds inside the croissant if you like.

Brownies

Preparation Time: 10 minutes

Cooking Time: 20 minutes

Servings: 2

Ingredients:

- ¼ cup all purpose flour
- ¼ teaspoon baking powder
- 1/3 cup cocoa powder
- ¼ cup butter
- ½ cup granulated sugar
- 1 egg, beaten
- Pinch salt

Method:

1. Spray baking pan with oil.
2. In a bowl, mix all the ingredients.
3. Pour mixture into the baking pan.
4. Set your air fryer to bake.
5. Cook at 350 degrees F for 18 to 20 minutes.

Serving Suggestions: Let cool for 10 minutes before slicing and serving.

Preparation & Cooking Tips: You can also top the brownies with chopped walnuts.

Apple Chips

Preparation Time: 10 minutes

Cooking Time: 12 minutes

Servings: 2

Ingredients:

- 2 apples, sliced thinly
- 2 teaspoons granulated sugar
- ½ teaspoon cinnamon

Method:

1. Coat apple slices with sugar and cinnamon.
2. Add these to the air fryer.
3. Choose bake setting.
4. Cook at 350 degrees F for 12 minutes, flipping two to three times.

Serving Suggestions: Serve with maple syrup.

Preparation & Cooking Tips: You can also serve these with marshmallows on top.

Caramelized Peaches

Preparation Time: 10 minutes

Cooking Time: 15 minutes

Servings: 2

Ingredients:

- 1 lb. peaches, sliced in half
- 1 tablespoon maple syrup
- ½ tablespoon coconut sugar
- ¼ teaspoon cinnamon powder

Method:

1. Brush peaches with maple syrup.
2. Sprinkle with coconut sugar and cinnamon.
3. Cook in the air fryer at 350 degrees F for 15 minutes.

Serving Suggestions: Serve with yogurt.

Preparation & Cooking Tips: You can omit the cinnamon powder if you like.

Blueberry Crumble

Preparation Time: 15 minutes

Cooking Time: 15 minutes

Servings: 4

Ingredients:

- ½ cup blueberries, sliced
- 1 apple, diced
- 2 tablespoons butter
- 2 tablespoons sugar
- ¼ cup rice flour
- ½ teaspoon cinnamon powder

Method:

1. Mix all the ingredients in a small baking pan.
2. Place inside the air fryer.
3. Choose bake setting.
4. Set it to 350 degrees F.
5. Cook for 15 minutes.

Serving Suggestions: Drizzle with honey before serving.

Preparation & Cooking Tips: You can also use strawberries in place of blueberries.

Apple Crisp

Preparation Time: 20 minutes

Cooking Time: 15 minutes

Servings: 2

Ingredients:

Apple crisp

- 2 apples, chopped
- 2 tablespoons brown sugar
- 1 teaspoon lemon juice
- 1 teaspoon cinnamon

Topping

- 2 tablespoons brown sugar
- 2 tablespoons flour
- 3 tablespoons oats
- 2 tablespoons cold butter, sliced into cubes
- Pinch salt

Method:

1. Set your air fryer to bake.
2. Preheat it to 350 degrees F.
3. Mix the apple crisp ingredients in a baking pan.
4. In a bowl, mix the topping ingredients.
5. Spread the toppings on top of the apple crisp.
6. Place inside the air fryer.
7. Cook for 15 minutes.

Serving Suggestions: Top with vanilla ice cream.

Preparation & Cooking Tips: Use freshly squeezed lemon juice.

Cinnamon Banana

Preparation Time: 10 minutes

Cooking Time: 5 minutes

Servings: 2

Ingredients:

- 2 bananas, sliced
- ¼ teaspoon cinnamon
- ½ teaspoon brown sugar
- 1 tablespoon granola

Method:

1. Toss the ingredients in a bowl.
2. Pour into a small baking pan.
3. Air fry at 400 degrees F for 5 minutes.

Serving Suggestions: Sprinkle toasted chopped nuts on top

Preparation & Cooking Tips: Don't forget to grease your baking pan before using.

Baked Apples & Raisins

Preparation Time: 10 minutes

Cooking Time: 20 minutes

Servings: 4

Ingredients:

- 4 apples, sliced
- 6 teaspoons raisins
- 2 teaspoons walnuts, chopped
- 2 teaspoons honey
- ½ teaspoon cinnamon powder

Method:

1. Mix all the ingredients in a small baking pan.
2. Place inside the air fryer.
3. Set it to bake.
4. Cook at 350 degrees F for 15 minutes.
5. Stir and cook for another 5 minutes.

Serving Suggestions: Serve while warm.

Preparation & Cooking Tips: Leftovers can be stored in the refrigerator for up to 3 days.

Grilled Pineapple

Preparation Time: 10 minutes

Cooking Time: 10 minutes

Servings: 4

Ingredients:

- 1 pineapple, sliced
- 4 tablespoons butter, melted
- ½ cup brown sugar
- 2 teaspoons cinnamon powder

Method:

1. Brush pineapple slices with butter.
2. Sprinkle with sugar and cinnamon powder.
3. Air fry at 400 degrees F for 10 minutes.

Serving Suggestions: Serve with vanilla ice cream.

Preparation & Cooking Tips: You can also use canned pineapple rings.

Chapter 10: 30-Day Menu Plan

Day 1

Breakfast: French toast strips

Lunch: Parmesan chicken breast

Dinner: Garlic butter steak with herbs

Day 2

Breakfast: Egg sandwich

Lunch: Orange chicken

Dinner: Cheeseburger

Day 3

Breakfast: Bagel

Lunch: Garlic parmesan chicken

Dinner: Beef mac & cheese

Day 4

Breakfast: Omelette

Lunch: Chicken tenders

Dinner: Steak with mashed cauliflower

Day 5

Breakfast: Fish & sweet potato chips

Lunch: Chicken strips with honey mustard

Dinner: Beef & asparagus

Day 6

Breakfast: Sweet potato hash

Lunch: Spicy chicken

Dinner: Beef & green beans

Day 7

Breakfast: Bacon & eggs

Lunch: Garlic herb chicken

Dinner: Roast beef

Day 8

Breakfast: Breakfast sausage patties

Lunch: Chicken Reuben

Dinner: Burger steak

Day 9

Breakfast: Cauliflower bites

Lunch: Pesto fish

Dinner: Country steak

Day 10

Breakfast: Mexican hash browns

Lunch: Lemon garlic fish fillet

Dinner: Parmesan pork chops

Day 11

Breakfast: Breakfast casserole

Lunch: Blackened tilapia

Dinner: Paprika pork chops with corn

Day 12

Breakfast: Egg rolls

Lunch: Shrimp bang bang

Dinner: Barbecue pork tenderloin

Day 13

Breakfast: Baked potatoes

Lunch: Honey glazed salmon

Dinner: Garlic pork chops with roasted broccoli

Day 14

Breakfast: Bacon & broccoli rice bowl

Lunch: Salmon with thyme & mustard

Dinner: Pork belly bites

Day 15

Breakfast: French toast strips

Lunch: Crispy fish fillet

Dinner: Mustard herbed pork chops

Day 16

Breakfast: Egg sandwich

Lunch: Garlic butter lobster tails

Dinner: Pork chops with creamy dip

Day 17

Breakfast: Bagel

Lunch: Garlic butter steak with herbs

Dinner: Tofu nuggets

Day 18

Breakfast: Omelette

Lunch: Cheeseburger

Dinner: Zucchini lasagna

Day 19

Breakfast: Fish & sweet potato chips

Lunch: Beef mac & cheese

Dinner: Onion rings

Day 20

Breakfast: Sweet potato hash

Lunch: Steak with mashed cauliflower

Dinner: Veggie rolls

Day 21

Breakfast: Bacon & eggs

Lunch: Beef & asparagus

Dinner: Vegetarian pizza

Day 22

Breakfast: Breakfast sausage patties

Lunch: Beef & green beans

Dinner: Brussels sprout chips

Day 23

Breakfast: Cauliflower bites

Lunch: Roast beef

Dinner: Spring rolls

Day 24

Breakfast: Mexican hash browns

Lunch: Tofu nuggets

Dinner: Parmesan chicken breast

Day 25

Breakfast: Breakfast casserole

Lunch: Zucchini lasagna

Dinner: Orange chicken

Day 26

Breakfast: Egg rolls

Lunch: Onion rings

Dinner: Garlic parmesan chicken

Day 27

Breakfast: Baked potatoes

Lunch: Veggie rolls

Dinner: Chicken tenders

Day 28

Breakfast: Bacon & broccoli rice bowl

Lunch: Vegetarian pizza

Dinner: Chicken strips with honey mustard

Day 29

Breakfast: Bagel

Lunch: Brussels sprout chips

Dinner: Spicy chicken

Day 30

Breakfast: Omelette

Lunch: Spring rolls

Dinner: Garlic herb chicken

Conclusion

The rapid changes in technology might make you feel like you are always chasing after what's trendy but having the PowerXL Air Fryer Grill in your kitchen might just be the one craze worth jumping into.

The convenient and low maintenance nature of this appliance will save you space, time and money in the long run. It allows you to go about other things while it does for you not one but eight cooking styles of a limitless selection of tasty healthy dishes.

Truly, the PowerXL Air Fryer Grill will literally and figuratively transform the air in your cooking and dining at home experience.

Made in the USA
Coppell, TX
27 December 2020